A PHOTOGRAPI ... THE

CANADIAN ROCKIES

Summerthought

Banff, Canada

A PHOTOGRAPHIC HISTORY OF THE CANADIAN ROCKIES

Published by
Summerthought

Summerthought Publishing
PO Box 2309
Banff, AB T1L 1C1
Canada
www.summerthought.com

We gratefully acknowledge the financial support of the Alberta Multimedia Development Fund.

Alberta Government

Library and Archives Canada Cataloguing in Publication

Hempstead, Andrew
A photographic history of the Canadian Rockies / Andrew Hempstead.

Includes index.
ISBN 978-1-926983-06-6

1. Rocky Mountains, Canadian (B.C. and Alta.)—History—Pictorial works. I. Title.

FC219.H463 2012 971.10022'2 C2012-900414-6

Design and production: Linda Petras
Printed in Canada by Friesens

PHOTO CREDITS

Summerthought Publishing would like to thank the following for permission to reproduce their archival images:

BC Archives: p. 50 (i-51558); p. 51 (i-21500); p. 57 (b-09408).

Eleanor Luxton Historical Foundation: p. 30-31; p. 69; p. 93 lower.

Glenbow Archives: p. 8 (NA-1909-5); p. 9 top (NA-2977-1); p. 10-11 (NA-1432-17); p. 38 (NA-3740-5; William Notman); p. 41 (NA-937-2; S.J. Thompson); p. 44 (NA-1408-19; Charles Horetzky); p. 45 top (NA-1679-12; Edgar Spurgeon); p. 52 (NA-678-1); p. 53 top (NA-1585-6); p. 63 (NA-3934-14); p. 64-65 (NA-1075-4); p. 70 (NA-2977-19); p. 82 (NB-32-7); p. 83 top (NB-32-33), lower (NA-4868-139).

Jasper-Yellowhead Museum & Archives: p. 16 lower (PA41-88); p. 45 lower (PA 18-3); p. 46 top (997.07.77.07), lower (89.36.262); p. 47 top (PA 18-22), lower (996.33.390); p. 58 (PA 101-3), p. 77 lower (000.34.249).

Whyte Museum of the Canadian Rockies: front cover (V469/1552; George Noble); p. 1 (V527/NG-124; Mary Schäffer); p. 4 (V263/NA-4910; Byron Harmon); p. 6 (V10/NA66-680); p. 9 lower (V484/NA66-345); p. 12 (V653/NA-1609; Vaux family); p. 13 top (V10/NA66-650; Boorne and May), lower (V265/NA66-267); p. 14-15 (V10/NA66-695; Boorne & May); p. 16 top (V263/NA-1157; Byron Harmon); p. 17 (V263/NA-0242; Byron Harmon); p. 18 (V138-lc-NA66-2471; William G. Barclay); p. 19 (V653/NG-255); p. 20 (V653/NG-737; Vaux family); p. 21 top (V653/NG-481; Vaux family), lower (NA66-236); p. 22 (V10/NA66-681; Boorne & May); p. 23 (V10/NA66-692; Boorne & May); p. 24 (V653/NA-103; Vaux family); p. 26-27 (V633/NA66-1796); p. 27 (V701-lc-232; John Woodruff); p. 28 top (NA-529-20), lower (V653/NA80-67; Vaux family); p. 29 (V86/NA66-1788); p. 31 (V484/NA29-334); p. 32 (V469/1131; George Noble); p. 33 top (V469/1097; George Noble), lower (V263/NA-3392); p. 35 (V92/NA66-1873; Malcolm Meades); p. 34 (NA66-1488); p. 39 (NA66-162); p. 40 (V469/993; George Noble); p. 41 (NA66-134; Bert Prendergast); p. 43 (V469/2691; George Noble); p. 48-49 (V263/NA-5308); p. 49 top (V701/LC-223); p. 53 lower (V91/NA66-2250); p. 54 (na66-1989); p. 55 top (V48/NA65-226), lower (NA66-459); p. 56 (V653/NG-26; Vaux family); p. 60 (V341/lc-NA66-1354; John Woodruff); p. 61 (V469/1859; George Noble); p. 62 (V469/955; George Noble); p. 64 (NA66-543; Walter D. Wilcox); p. 66 (V469/1835); p. 67 top (V90/PC-1-NA66-1962), lower (V92/NG3-3); p. 68 (V341/lc-NA66-1359; John Woodruff); p. 71 top (V287/lc-NA66-2387), lower (V653/NA-1621; Vaux family); p. 72 (V469/2590; George Noble); p. 73 (V263/NA-5061; Byron Harmon); p. 74 top (V469/2343; George Noble), lower (V469/479; George Noble); p. 75 (V469/1002; George Noble); p. 76 top (V469/999; George Noble), lower (V469/1029; George Noble); p. 77 top (NA66-2419; F.H. Slark); p. 78 (V469/618; George Noble); p. 79 top (V469/2044; George Noble), lower (V263/NA-5320; Byron Harmon); p. 80 (V263/NA-5235; Byron Harmon); p. 81 (V469/931; George Noble); p. 84 top (V701/lc-5; Charles Thompson), lower (NA66-186); p. 85 (V200/NA66-1818; Walter Wilcox); p. 86 (V263/NA-0936); p. 87 (V226/lc-NA66-2407); p. 88-89 (V263/NA-153; Byron Harmon); p. 90 top (V701/LC-36), lower (V85/NA66-577); p. 91 (V120/NA66-1767); p. 92 (V529/lc-3-NA66-198; Howard A. Chapman); p. 93 top (V48/427; Elliott Barnes); p. 98-99 (V469/1552; George Noble); p. 95 top (NA66-412), lower (NA66-413); back cover (v683-na66-2396).

Contents

A diver plunges into the Terrace Pool at the Chateau Lake Louise.

Introduction

Beautiful lakes, snowcapped peaks, endless glaciers and icefields, colourful alpine meadows, and an abundance of wildlife. While these are the elements the Canadian Rockies are best known for, the region also has a colourful and intriguing human history that has been recorded in various mediums.

Human habitation of the Canadian Rockies began long before the first Europeans arrived. It is thought the Kootenay (also spelt Kootenai) were the first human beings to arrive in the Canadian Rockies, entering the Columbia River Valley around 10,000 years ago and crossing the mountains to hunt on the Kootenay Plains. The movement of humans into the mountains from the east was much more recent, with Assiniboine (known today as Stoney) people reaching the foothills region a few hundred years ago. While pictographs created by these earliest visitors are the only visual record of pre-European contact, early photographers found willing models in the Stoney and many photographic images from the late 1800s and early 1900s reflect the traditions and customs of these people.

In 1754, from a ridge near present Red Deer, Anthony Henday became the first white man to view the Canadian Rockies. In 1807, David Thompson crossed the mountains by travelling up the North Saskatchewan River from Rocky Mountain House, and descending from Howse Pass to the Columbia River. A half-century later, Captain John Palliser explored many of the watersheds leading into the mountains, including one trip up the Bow River and over Vermilion Pass. While there is no photographic record of these expeditions, it was these earliest explorers that opened up the region to those that would follow.

Railway crew on hand car, 1888.

Trains

In the 1860s, with a movement to push for Canadian independence gaining ground, the British government passed legislation establishing the Dominion of Canada. At that time, life in the North-West Territories, as most of what is now western Canada was then known, was primitive. There were no laws, and no outpost held more than a couple of dozen residents. In an effort to solidify the region's British sovereignty, British Columbia joined the Dominion on the condition that the federal government committed to building a railway to link the fledgling province with the rest of the country. While it proved to be an essential ingredient to the success of settling the West, a railway was mostly regarded by the eastern provinces as unnecessary and uneconomical.

Many routes across the Canadian Rockies were considered by the Canadian Pacific Railway, but Kicking Horse Pass, surveyed by Major A. B. Rogers in 1881, got the final nod. The rail line and its construction camps pushed into the mountains from the east, reaching Siding 29 (known today as Banff) early in the fall of 1883, Holt City (Lake Louise) a couple of months later, then crossing the Continental Divide and reaching what is now the village of Field in the summer of 1884. The following year, on November 7, 1885, the final spike was laid west of Rogers Pass at Craigellachie, opening up the lanes of commerce between British Columbia and the rest of the Canada. A second, more northerly route through Edmonton and Jasper, was completed by the Grand Trunk Pacific Railway in 1914.

With two expensive rail lines in place, the government set about putting them to use by settling the land and encouraging tourists to visit the thriving resort towns of Banff and Jasper. Roads were built and industries—including logging, mining, farming, and tourism—started to develop.

Canmore

As the railway pushed westward into the Canadian Rockies, the first major divisional point was Canmore, which was named for a Scottish town. By 1886, a ramshackle community had been established along the tracks (pictured), but at this time there was no hint at the riches of coal that would see the town thrive in later years.

Banff Railway Station

The original Banff Railway Station (above) as it looked in 1888, the year that the Banff Springs Hotel opened. The station was an important part of town life for many decades and was the only link to the outside world.

Holt City
When construction of the transcontinental rail line reached what is now Lake Louise in 1884, a rough-and-tumble construction camp known as "Holt City" sprang up in the wilderness.

Kicking Horse Pass
West of Lake Louise, the original rail line had a gradient of 4.5% as it descended from Kicking Horse Pass. After two decades, this treacherous stretch of track was replaced by the famous Spiral Tunnels, which were completed in 1909 after three years of construction. The new routing comprised two tunnels that looped through Cathedral Mountain and Mount Ogden. The tunnels made a circular route, emerging around 20 meters (66 feet) below the point where they entered the mountains, and thereby reducing the gradient by half.

Field

As construction of the rail line moved westward, camps were erected to house and feed railway workers. One such settlement was Field (above), which was named for Cyrus Field, sponsor of the first transatlantic communication cable. The workers pictured (right) are shown constructing the line through Kicking Horse Canyon, west of Field, which proved to be just as challenging as the section across Kicking Horse Pass.

Mountain Creek Bridge
Immediately west of the Canadian Rockies, the rugged Selkirk Mountains provided yet more challenges for railway engineers and workers. The Mountain Creek Bridge, one of eight bridges through these mountains, needed around two million board feet of lumber and was at the time one of the world's largest wooden structures.

Summit City
Jasper had already been declared a park when the Grand Trunk Pacific Railway was constructed as a rival to the more southern Canadian Pacific Railway. During construction, workers were housed in temporary camps such as Summit City (right) at the Yellowhead Pass. The most important stop along the line was Jasper (below), at a railway station that still serves as a stop along the transcontinental rail line.

Mine Railways
Various mining operations through the Canadian Rockies relied on the railway for transportation. A concentration of mines was in the Kicking Horse Valley, where lead and zinc were extracted from high on the slopes of Mt. Stephen and transported to the valley floor in small coal cars. Pictured is the precarious access road to one of these mines, the Monarch, which began operation in 1912.

Winter in the Canadian Rockies
Rotary snowplows, similar to the one pictured above, were developed to help clear the snow, which quickly accumulated through the winter months. When this proved inadequate, expensive "snow sheds" (opposite) in the Selkirk Mountains, were constructed where snowfall and avalanche risk were highest.

Mount Stephen House
In an effort to recoup some of the money spent in laying the railway through the Canadian Rockies, William Cornelius Van Horne, general manager of the Canadian Pacific Railway, ordered construction of dining rooms and hotels to serve visitors using the railway. One of these was Mount Stephen House, in Field, which was completed in 1886. It was luxurious in all respects—from its elegant gas lights to fine china—but unlike iconic railway hotels in Banff and Lake Louise, no longer exists.

Glacier House

Another dining room no longer in existence is Glacier House, at Rogers Pass, which was built in 1886 as a place where trains could stop to allow travellers to have a meal. Eventually rooms were added allowing for overnight stays. In this image (right), staff from Glacier House pose for the photographer.

Moberly House
While some railway construction camps evolved into bustling towns, others, such as Moberly House at the mouth of the Blaeberry River near present-day Golden, were abandoned as soon as workers moved on.

Donald
Engine 316 at Donald, British Columbia in 1887. Donald, west of Golden, was originally a divisional point for the Canadian Pacific Railway, but was abandoned for Revelstoke less than a decade after the railway was completed. Those interested in the history of train travel in the Canadian Rockies will enjoy visits to the nearby Revelstoke Railway Museum and Cranbrook's Canadian Museum of Rail Travel.

Illecillewaet, once a bustling town, has long since disappeared.

Towns

In the late 1880s, after the Canadian Pacific Railway had been completed, the Canadian Rockies region was a vast wilderness accessible only by rail. The parks and the landscape they encompassed were considered economic resources to be exploited rather than as national treasures to be preserved. Logging, hunting, and mining were permitted inside park boundaries; all but Kootenay National Park had mines operating within them for many years (the last mine, in Yoho National Park, closed in 1952). Today, five national parks protect much of the Canadian Rockies, with the towns of Banff and Jasper at the heart of their respectively named parks.

Many of the region's earliest towns were built around mining operations, including Bankhead, Anthracite, Pocahontas, and Oil City, all of which have long since disappeared. Canmore, on the other hand, where mining began in 1887, continues to thrive. The region's most famous town, Banff, was developed around hot springs that had been discovered by railway workers. With the idea of developing a European-style spa resort, the government surveyed a townsite and encouraged the CPR to build a world-class hotel. Meanwhile to the north, the town of Jasper started as a construction camp, but became popular as a tourist destination in the early 1900s.

Banff Avenue businesses
After completion of the railway in 1883, many wooden buildings were constructed along Banff Avenue. One of these was the Park Store, which was owned by Dave White. Over the years, White replaced the original structure with a red brick building that stands to this day, with his name adorning the south-facing wall.

Banff Avenue
Although much has changed since this photo of Banff Avenue was taken in 1887 (left), one constant has been Cascade Mountain, which rises majestically to the north.

Banff businesses
After being surveyed in 1886, Banff Avenue became the town's main street. The first buildings were simple wood-frame structures with false fronts. One such business was Wilson & Fear, one of the town's many "curio stores" that stocked a wide range of merchandise (right) appealing to both locals and tourists.

Banff's Post Office
Banff's first post office was this primitive log cabin on the east side of Banff Avenue that operated through the 1890s.

Lake Minnewanka
Lake Minnewanka has always been a popular spot for Banff locals in summer. A hotel was built beside the lake in 1886 and by 1912 streets had been laid out at the "Summer Village" and tour boats were operating up and down the lake. When the present dam was built in 1941, the townsite was flooded, leaving the village nothing but a memory that is today only visited by divers.

Banff Winter Carnival
The Banff Winter Carnival was devised as a way to keep the locals entertained during winter and also to attract tourists in the off-season. A highlight was an Ice Palace on Banff Avenue (opposite, top) while ski jumping, ski racing, figure-skating (above), and cross-country skiing attracted competitors from throughout the region. Other carnival spectacles became annual traditions including a toboggan run extending from Tunnel Mountain to the Bow River and ice carving (opposite).

DAVE WHITE & CO.

Visiting royalty
The town of Banff has always been a popular stop for celebrities and royalty, including King George VI and Queen Elizabeth, who stayed at the Banff Springs Hotel in 1939. Jim Brewster, who was assigned as their chauffeur (above; holding the reigns), invited the royal couple to stop by his home for afternoon tea, to which they kindly agreed. Local legend has it that Jim failed to inform his wife of the plan, and arrived unannounced with the King and Queen of England.

Skiing at Sunshine (opposite)
In March 1929, two Banff boys, Cliff White and Cyril Paris, returned from an area known as Sunshine with stories of deep snow and excellent skiing conditions. In the ensuing years, many locals followed in their footsteps and by 1934 paying guests were staying in a small log cabin overlooking the best runs.

Banff townsite, 1887
Looking down at the Banff townsite from Tunnel Mountain in 1887, Banff Avenue dominates as the main thoroughfare. On the south side of the Bow River, the road to the hot springs is also obvious.

Spray Avenue
One of Banff's busiest streets at the turn of the last century was Spray Avenue, which linked the townsite with the Banff Springs Hotel.

Canmore
This 1889 photo looking south across Canmore from the hoodoos shows early town buildings concentrated along the railway line. Canmore's first coal mine began operation two years earlier on the south side of the Bow River.

Canmore Railway Bridge
This photo was taken in the early 1900s looking down the Bow River where it flows through Canmore. The bridge in the foreground, now part of the town's hiking trail system, was used to transport coal from the mines to the main Canadian Pacific Railway line.

The Shareholders Cabin
The Shareholders Cabin was built in 1914 as a place for mine shareholders to stay when they visited Canmore. Having undergone extensive renovations, this impressive log building still stands in a prime location across the Bow River from downtown.

Canada Day
Canada Day has always been a popular event in Canmore. This photo shows the 1925 parade.

Three Sisters
Canmore's Three Sisters remain a local landmark, well over a century since this photo (above) was taken in the 1880s. By the 1920s (opposite), the highway had reached Canmore and the town had established itself as a coal-mining centre.

30-051

Jasper House
Jasper House, as photographed by surveyor Charles Horetzky in 1872. Operated by Jasper Hawes for the Hudson's Bay Company, this remote trading post was located along the Athabasca River east of present-day Jasper. It served as an important stopping place for traders and explorers from 1825 until a couple of years after this photograph was taken.

Jasper grows
In 1911, the Grand Trunk Pacific Railway chose the present-day site of Jasper as a major station. Stores were opened, accommodation built for park staff, and by 1914, when the rail line was completed, the town had a population of 125, and even its own firehall (right).

Park Administration Building
Now home to the Jasper Visitor Centre, the Park Administration Building is a local landmark. Designed by architect A. M. Calderon and completed in 1914, it was built using local materials and intended to give a positive first impression for rail travellers who alighted from the nearby railway station.

Jasper Rodeo
Rodeos aren't usually associated with the Canadian Rockies, but the Jasper Rodeo has been a popular gathering in that town since the inaugural event in 1926. Pictured is Slim Henry riding Skyhigh to first place in the 1937 rodeo.

Jasper townsite
This image (above) depicts Jasper's main thoroughfare in 1926, which by that time had a permanent look. The second building from the left was originally owned by the Jackman family and is now home to Jasper Camera and Gift. By 1930 (right), Jasper as a town had taken shape, with streets laid out as you find them today.

P. BURNS & COMPANY
LIMITED
J. A. BUCKHAM

Prospecting
A prospector at Golden in 1884. Unlike the name may suggest, there never has been any gold found at Golden. Instead, the town's name was coined in an attempt to outshine a boomtown to the east near Banff which had called itself Silver City.

Golden
Unlike many other construction camps along the Canadian Pacific Railway, Golden thrived long after itinerant construction workers had moved. This photo looking down on town was taken by Byron Harmon in 1931.

Athalmer
Once a bustling town on the northern shore of Lake Windermere, Athalmer has long since been lost to time, although the original railway station is preserved at Windermere Valley Museum, which overlooks the former townsite.

Invermere
What is most striking about this aerial photograph looking north across Invermere is the date—it was taken as recently as 1968.

John George "Kootenai" Brown
John George "Kootenai" Brown acquired his nickname through close association with the Kootenay (today's preferred spelling) people, hunting buffalo and wolves with them until the animals had all but disappeared. Brown built a cabin by Upper Waterton Lake in 1869, becoming the valley's first permanent resident. When a reserve was set aside in 1895, Brown was employed as its first warden. In 1911, the area was declared a national park and Brown, age 71, was appointed its superintendent. He continued to push for an expansion of park boundaries until his final retirement at age 75.

Oil City
The short-lived Rocky Mountain Development Company, which struck oil in what is now Waterton Lakes National Park in 1901, was the first producing oil well in western Canada.

Waterton townsite
Looking across Upper Waterton Lake in 1935, Waterton townsite can be seen on the low-lying land to the right while the silhouette of the Prince of Wales Hotel clearly visible on a bluff.

Silver City
A plaque beside the Bow Valley Parkway in Banff National Park marks the site of Silver City, once a boomtown in the shadow of Castle Mountain. In the 1880s, five mines were operating and the town had six hotels, numerous general stores, two real estate offices, and a railway station. Two men, Patton and Pettigrew, salted their mine with gold and silver ore to attract further investment, but then vanished. By 1887, investment in the town ceased, mines closed, the prospectors and businessmen left, and most buildings were dismantled. Only one man refused to leave Silver City. His name was James Smith, but he was known to everyone as Joe. In 1887, when Silver City came under the jurisdiction of the National Parks Service, Joe was allowed to remain. It wasn't until 1937 that he finally moved to a Calgary retirement home, where he died soon after.

Bankhead

Along what is now Lake Minnewanka Road in Banff National Park, Bankhead was once a thriving coal-mining town of 1,000 residents. Coal was extracted from the mid-slopes of Cascade Mountain and transported by coal cars to the valley floor, where this tipple (right) sorted and processed the raw ore. When the mine closed in 1922, all the buildings were moved or demolished. Some foundations remain, include those of Holy Trinity Church, which can be seen in the distance in this 1910 photo (below).

Anthracite
Many towns through the Canadian Rockies have disappeared. Some began as rough-and-tumble mining camps, including Anthracite, a coal-mining town between present-day Banff and Canmore. It flourished between 1896 and 1904, with a population that peaked at around 300.

Fort Steele
When gold was discovered along Wild Horse Creek in 1865, the Columbia Valley was flooded with hopeful miners. The town of Fort Steele grew to be the largest in the valley, its main street (pictured in 1898) lined with businesses that have been re-created at today's Fort Steele Heritage Town, north of Cranbrook.

Women skiers at Jasper.

Tourism

With an expensive rail line in place, the Canadian Pacific Railway began encouraging visitors to the mountains by building grand mountain resorts: Mount Stephen House in 1886, the Banff Springs Hotel in 1888, a lodge at Lake Louise in 1890, and Emerald Lake Lodge in 1902. Knowledgeable locals, some of whom had been used as guides and outfitters during railway construction, offered their services to the tourists the railway brought. Tom Wilson, Bill Peyto, Jimmy Simpson, and Jim and Bill Brewster are synonymous with this era, and their names grace everything from pubs to mountain peaks.

Recreational mountaineering has been popular in the Canadian Rockies since the late 1800s, when European and American alpinists began making first ascents. Many early climbers were inexperienced and ill-equipped, but first ascents were nevertheless made on peaks that today are still considered difficult. In 1894, Walter Wilcox and Samuel Allen, two Yale schoolmates, spent the summer climbing in the Lake Louise area, making successful first ascents of Mount Temple and Mount Aberdeen, extraordinary achievements considering their lack of experience and proper equipment. After Philip Stanley Abbot became North America's first mountaineering fatality in 1896, the Canadian Pacific Railway began employing Swiss guides to make the sport safer.

One of the major changes that has occurred since the first tourists began arriving in the Canadian Rockies is the way the complex relationship between humans and wildlife has been managed. Today, the trend favours the wildlife, but early in the history of the Canadian Rockies' parks, the operating strategy clearly favoured the visitor, as you will discover in this chapter.

Cave and Basin

On November 8, 1883, three workers—Franklin McCabe and William and Thomas McCardell—went prospecting for gold on their day off from construction of the rail line through the Bow Valley. After crossing the Bow River by raft, they came across a warm stream and traced it to its source at a small basin of warm water. Nearby, they detected a sulphurous smell permeating from a hole in the ground. Nervously, one of the three men lowered himself into the hole and came across a subterranean pool of aqua-green warm water. The three men had found not gold, but something just as precious—a hot mineral spring that in time would attract wealthy customers from around the world. Word of the discovery soon got out, and the government encouraged visitors to the Cave and Basin (pictured opposite in 1890) as a source of revenue to support the new railway. In 1914 architect Walter Painter designed an imposing stone bathhouse (above), which has been extensively restored and is protected as a national historic site.

Radium Hot Springs

Radium Hot Springs, in Kootenay National Park, was discovered many centuries ago by the Kootenay people, who, like today's visitors, came to enjoy the hot, odourless water that gushes out of the ground. Originally known as Sinclair Hot Springs, Englishman Roland Stuart purchased the springs for $160 in 1890 and built rough concrete pools to contain the water. Today the water is diverted from its natural course into the commercial pools, including one that is Canada's largest.

Miette Hot Springs
Miette Hot Springs was a major attraction for early tourists visiting Jasper National Park. In 1910, a packhorse trail was built up to the remote springs and a bathhouse was constructed (pictured). The original hand-hewn log structure was replaced in the 1930s with pools that remained in use until new facilities were built in 1985.

Banff Springs Hotel
Known as "the Castle," the Banff Springs Hotel was completed in 1888 and at the time was the world's largest hotel. Pictured above and right is the original wooden hotel.

Hotel Bretton Hall

Dr. Robert G. Brett, a medical practitioner for the Canadian Pacific Railway, saw the potential for a health resort affiliated with the hot springs and opened the Banff Sanitarium in 1887. It was renamed Hotel Bretton Hall in 1922 but burned down in 1933. Today, the Park Administration Building stands on the site.

The Brewsters

Few guides in Banff were as well known as Jim (right) and Bill Brewster. In 1892, before they were even teenagers, they were hired by the Banff Springs Hotel to take guests to local attractions. As their reputation as guides grew, they built a thriving business. By 1900, they had their own livery and outfitting company (below). Their other business interests included a trading post, the original Mount Royal Hotel, a ski lodge in Sunshine Meadows, and the hotel at the Columbia Icefield.

Fishing
Fishing has always been a major tourist attraction in the Canadian Rockies, with many lakes and rivers stocked with trout. This photo of a woman fishing in the Bow River dates to 1890.

Banff Indian Days
In 1894, heavy rains washed out several railway bridges, halting train traffic in Banff. To entertain stranded travellers, Stoney people from nearby Morley were bought in to put on a dance demonstration. The event proved so popular that they were invited back for Dominion Day until 1907 when Banff Indian Days was launched as its own annual event. A colourful parade along Banff Avenue (above) marked the beginning of several days of singing, dancing, and native athletic competitions.

Lake Louise

The first accommodation at Lake Louise was a simple log cabin (opposite) that opened for guests in 1890. It featured a veranda, sitting room, kitchen, and one bedroom. In its early years less than 100 guests—mostly climbers and artists—would visit over the entire summer season. By the early 1900s, Lake Louise Chalet (above) had expanded greatly and in 1909, two Tudor-style timber wings were added (right).

Plain of the Six Glaciers Teahouse
Constructed in the 1920s by the Canadian Pacific Railway, Plain of the Six Glaciers Teahouse still operates today—serving light refreshments to hikers who make the long trek up from Lake Louise.

Moraine Lake

One of the most beautiful lakes in the Canadian Rockies is Moraine Lake. Within a decade of its discovery by Walter Wilcox in 1899, a trail from Lake Louise had been constructed and a teahouse built on the lakeshore. In 1922, cabins were built, with more added through the years. In 1988, architect Arthur Erickson transformed the complex into elegant Moraine Lake Lodge, one of the world's great mountain retreats.

Icefields Parkway
Construction of the mountainous Icefields Parkway between Lake Louise and Jasper began in 1931, with crews working toward each other from both ends. The ambitious 230-kilometre (143-mile)-long project was completed in 1939. Today's Icefields Parkway follows much of the original roadbed, and was paved in the late 1950s. Travellers still enjoy the same spectacular mountain scenery as early travelers, including views across to Mt. Temple (left) and north to distinctive Mt. Chephren (below).

Num-Ti-Jah Lodge
When it was built by legendary mountain man Jimmy Simpson in the 1920s, Num-Ti-Jah Lodge, on the shore of Bow Lake, was only accessible by horse from Lake Louise. When the Icefields Parkway reach Bow Lake in 1937, Simpson began upgrading the lodge with more rooms and a distinctive log and stone exterior that remains as appealing today as it did over 70 years ago.

Icefields Parkway through Jasper
The Swiss-influenced Columbia Icefield Chalet (left) opened in 1940, with early tourists exploring the nearby Athabasca Glacier on horseback. Further north, Sunwapta Falls (pictured below in 1940) has always been a popular natural attraction for visitors.

Jasper Park Lodge
In the same traditions as the Banff Springs Hotel, Jasper Park Lodge has been the premier accommodation in that park since it opened in 1921. The original resort comprised a single-storey structure, reputed to be the largest log building in the world, surrounded by log bungalows. In the main building was a lounge (pictured) and dining room.

Maligne Canyon Tea Room
Maligne Canyon has been one of Jasper's most popular attractions for over 100 years. In 1927, this log tea room overlooking the top of the canyon opened on the site of the present-day building.

Banff-Windermere Highway
Construction of the Banff-Windermere Highway through the rugged terrain of Kootenay National Park took almost a decade. Near Radium Hot Springs, Sinclair Canyon (pictured) had been eroded by the fast-flowing waters of Sinclair Creek, but was not wide enough for the road. After dynamiting the canyon and building the road over the top of the creek, the gap was wide enough for the two-lane highway as it exists today.

Kicking Horse Trail

Originally known as the Kicking Horse Trail, a road through Yoho National Park was completed in 1926 (right), but it wasn't until 1958 that the route was officially recognized. It is now the Trans-Canada Highway, although much of the original roadbed within the park has been bypassed, including the bridge in Kicking Horse Canyon pictured below.

Yoho Valley
Scenery is only part of the fun for drivers traversing Yoho Valley Road. Engineers were forced to include two very tight switchbacks (above) that to this day force buses to reverse through the mid-section. Snowfall in the valley is very high. Instead of waiting for the snow to melt, a tunnel would be cleared through the snow (opposite), allowing vehicles to reach Takakkaw Falls in spring.

Prince of Wales Hotel
Waterton's best-known landmark, the Prince of Wales Hotel, is a seven-storey gabled structure that has changed little in appearance since it took its first guests in 1927. It was another grand mountain resort financed by a railway, except, unlike those in Banff and Jasper, it had no rail link. It was built as part of a chain of lodgings in Glacier National Park, with early guests transported to the hotel by bus from the Great Northern Railway in Montana.

Akamina Parkway
The Akamina Parkway is one of the few roads penetrating Waterton Lakes National Park. Constructed in the 1920s, it allowed visitors to easily reach Cameron Lake, where fishing was the most popular activity.

Swiss guides

A rescue party (left) rests above Lake Louise while retrieving the body of Philip Stanley Abbot, who became North America's first climbing fatality in 1896. After his untimely death, the Canadian Pacific Railway hired Swiss mountaineers (below and opposite) as a way to promote adventure tourism and to ensure the safety of visitors. Based at mountain hotels in Banff, Lake Louise, Golden, and Rogers Pass, these guides made hundreds of first ascents in the Canadian Rockies.

Conrad Kain
Conrad Kain pictured leading a party to the summit of Mount Resplendent in 1913. Kain, an Austrian, was an official guide for the Alpine Club of Canada. He was credited with around 50 first ascents in the Canadian Rockies and Selkirk Mountains, but is best known as the first to reach the summit of Mount Robson, the highest mountain in the Canadian Rockies.

Trail Riders of the Canadian Rockies
In 1923, an eclectic group of outdoor enthusiasts—including noted wildlife artist Carl Rungius and Dr. Charles D. Walcott, secretary of the Smithsonian Institute—set off on an organized horseback ride to help promote the Canadian Rockies. Known today as the Trail Riders of the Canadian Rockies, the non-profit organization continues to thrive. Like they have for over 80 years, riders camp in tepees, feast on hearty camp cooking, and enjoy western-style entertainment, such as that provided in 1935 by Wilf Carter (pictured).

Alpine Club of Canada (following pages)
A 1914 Alpine Club of Canada outing silhouetted against the Yoho Glacier. This mountaineering club was formed in 1906 and is today headquartered in Canmore.

Tom Wilson
Employed by the Canadian Pacific Railway on an early survey team, Tom Wilson is credited with being the first non-native to set eyes on Lake Louise. He went on to operate a successful outfitting business, exploring the Yoho Valley and the area around Mount Assiniboine, while also mentoring the likes of Bill Peyto and Jimmy Simpson. After officially retiring, he was employed by the Banff Springs Hotel to entertain guests with stories from the "old days."

"Wild" Bill Peyto
One of the Canadian Rockies' greatest guides and also one of the region's most infamous characters was Bill Peyto, whose distinctive dress sense—a tilted sombrero, fringed buckskin coat, cartridge belt, hunting knife, and six-shooter—had him looking more like a gunslinger than a mountain man.

Park wardens
For over a century, wardens have been patrolling the parks of the Canadian Rockies. Pictured above is warden Jack Giddie surveying his territory from the summit of Mount Burgess, Yoho National Park, in 1924.

Banff Park Museum
Tourists visiting the Canadian Rockies in the early 1900s were eager to see wildlife without actually having to venture into the wilderness. To fill this need, the Government Museum, filled with taxidermied animals, was constructed on Banff Avenue. Adjacent to the museum was the Banff Zoo, which kept more than 60 species of animals. The zoo is long gone, but the museum, now operating as the Banff Park Museum, is an interesting link to the park's past.

Animal Paddock
Many animals were caged at the Animal Paddock, at the base of Cascade Mountain, including this cougar, photographed in 1907.

Buffalo Paddock
Beside the Animal Paddock was the Buffalo Paddock, which was built to enclose a herd of bison, including "Sir Donald" (right). A small herd of buffalo remained until 1997, when the fences were removed to create a wildlife corridor.

Changing attitudes

In addition to the changing needs of park visitors, over the last century human-wildlife relationships are now managed very differently. For a long time, feeding bears was considered part of the "wilderness" experience, and as recently as the 1960s, tourists were encouraged to watch bears feast on garbage at local dumps.

Index